STERLING CHILDREN'S BOOKS
New York

An Imprint of Sterling Publishing Co., Inc.
1166 Avenue of the Americas
New York, NY 10036

ISBN 978-1-4549-2236-0

Distributed in Canada by Sterling Publishing Co., Inc.
c/o Canadian Manda Group, 664 Annette Street
Toronto, Ontario, Canada M6S 2C8
Distributed in the United Kingdom by GMC Distribution Services
Castle Place, 166 High Street, Lewes, East Sussex, England BN7 1XU
Distributed in Australia by NewSouth Books
45 Beach Street, Coogee, NSW 2034, Australia

For information about custom editions, special sales, and premium and corporate purchases, please contact Sterling Special Sales at 800-805-5489 or specialsales@sterlingpublishing.com.

Manufactured in China

Lot #:

2 4 6 8 10 9 7 5 3 1

03/17

www.sterlingpublishing.com

AMERICAN MUSEUM ᵒꜰ NATURAL HISTORY

Baby Dolphin's First Swim

STERLING CHILDREN'S BOOKS
New York

A baby dolphin is born in the ocean. A baby dolphin is called a calf. He stays close to his mother for food and protection.

The ocean is a big place for a small dolphin. There is so much to explore!

The baby dolphin rises to the surface of the water and takes his first breath. He breathes through a hole on the top of his head, called a blowhole.

Dolphins are mammals and, like other mammals, they need to breathe air. They hold their breath underwater. Some dolphins can hold their breath for up to ten minutes!

The mother dolphin whistles to her baby. The baby learns to recognize his mother's call. He will eventually learn to whistle back.

Dolphins communicate by whistling, clicking, squawking, and squeaking. They make different noises when they're excited, scared, or happy. Dolphins can also communicate without making any noise at all. Their movements—a flip of the fin or a slap of the tail—often say a lot.

The baby dolphin is hungry. His tongue forms a straw shape so he can drink milk from his mother without drinking any salt water.

Calves rely on their mother's milk for up to three years.

They are able to drink and swim at the same time.

The baby dolphin's mother is hungry, too. She leaps out of the water and catches a tasty fish.

Dolphins eat all kinds of fish. Depending on where they live, they eat salmon, herring, and mackerel. They also eat shrimp and squid. Dolphins swallow their food whole, without chewing it.

Dolphins swim in groups called pods. The baby dolphin is the newest member of the pod! Dolphin pods can vary in size, typically ranging from two to forty members. Some pods become so large, they include thousands of dolphins!

The pod protects the baby dolphin.

The pod swims fast!

Dolphins have sleek bodies that help
them move through the water.

One day, the baby dolphin will be able to swim without the protection of his mother.

But for now, the baby dolphin swims with his mother, matching his movements with hers.

The dolphins jump into the air and land in the water.

Splash!

The baby dolphin learns more and
more about the ocean as he grows.

Dolphins are some of the smartest animals in the world. They have large brains and—when trained— can imitate humans. For example when a person claps, a dolphin can clap back!

Danger! A shark approaches!
Sharks are the dolphin's enemy.

The baby dolphin swims closer to his mother.

The size of the pod scares the shark. The shark

eventually swims away.

The dolphin's mother is hungry again and goes searching for food. While the mother is gone, the baby dolphin's "aunt" takes care of him. The "aunt" is another female dolphin in the pod.

All the female dolphins in the pod help care for the young.

The baby dolphin is tired. He needs a nap. He dozes off next to his mother.

Dolphins take many short naps. When they sleep, their brains are only half-resting. The alert part of the brain keeps the dolphin breathing and aware of danger.

The sun sets over the ocean. The baby dolphin's first day is over. Tomorrow will be another adventure.

Meet the Expert

My name is **Neil Duncan**, and I am a biologist.
I work for the Department of Mammalogy at
the American Museum of Natural History in
New York City. As the collections manager,
I get to work with all kinds of animal specimens
that have been gathered from around the world.

The natural world has always been a passion
of mine, and I have traveled all over the world to
study animals. In California, I researched small
forest carnivores called fishers and martens.
In the Bahamas, Belize, and Papua New Guinea,
I worked alongside other biologists surveying
the biodiversity of those areas. Currently,
I am involved with the Gotham Coyote Project,
studying coyotes as they expand their range
throughout the boroughs of New York City
and into Long Island, where I grew up.